A horse is a thing of such beauty...
none will tire of looking at him
as long as he displays himself in his splendor.

–Xenophon

Horse, thou are truly a creature without equal,
for thou fliest without wings and conquerest
without a sword.

–The Koran

The Kentucky Horse Park

A Real Kentucky Horse Farm Experience

The Kentucky Horse Park is a blend of old and new, respecting both honored traditions of the Bluegrass horse country and modern innovation. Officially opened to the public on November 30, 1978, the Park today continues to live up to its stated purpose

...to provide a quality informational, recreational and educational experience, with the horse as its theme, for Kentuckians and visitors from throughout the world. As the only Park in the world dedicated to the horse, it offers visitors a chance to see a variety of breeds of horse in their daily routines, against a background of an immaculately kept Kentucky horse farm.

The Kentucky Horse Park is a fascinating place where over one thousand acres of land are devoted to the horse and the important role it has played in the history of man. For anyone who admires the horse, a day at the Park can be the experience of a lifetime.

Visitors are greeted at the Park by the large bronze statue that marks the grave of the legendary Man o' War. The fascinating world of the horse comes alive through the exciting introductory film, "Thou Shalt Fly Without Wings," presented daily in the Visitor Information Center.

Two world-class museums can be found on the Park grounds, the International Museum of the Horse and the American Saddlebred Museum. The International Museum of the Horse is the largest and most comprehensive equestrian museum in the world, dedicated to telling the intriguing story of the horse and its relationship with man. State-of-the-art technology helps compliment an outstanding collection of information and artifacts, producing a truly unique and enjoyable museum experience. The American Saddlebred Museum concentrates on Kentucky's native breed and takes the visitor into the exciting world of the show ring with this historically influential breed.

Beyond the walls of the Museum, one can witness the day-to-day workings of a Kentucky horse farm. Watch as the Park's staff performs the daily chores of feeding, grooming and exercising the Park's hundred plus horses. Experience the sights and sounds of a blacksmith's shop as the Park's farrier shows his iron-pounding craft and practices the age-old art of horseshoeing.

The Park offers everyone the opportunity for hands-on experience with the horse on a trail ride or a horse drawn trolley or carriage tour of the Park grounds or by participating in one of the many education programs. From Mid-March through October the Park comes alive with the color, sound and excitement of the show ring. Twice daily the Breeds Barn hosts the Parade of Breeds, a presentation of selected horses highlighting the unique history and character of the some 40 different breeds that reside at the Park. The Hall of Champions is home to an elite group of horses representing Thoroughbred, Standardbred and Quarter Horse racing and past stars of the Saddlebred show ring which are presented three times daily.

Besides the daily activities, the Park is home for a full schedule of world class equestrian competitions including annual events like the Rolex Kentucky Three-Day Event, the High Hope Steeplechase and the Egyptian Event. The Park also hosts soccer tournaments, dog shows, concerts and special after hour programs throughout the year. The Christmas season comes alive with a spectacular light display featuring both Christmas and equestrian displays. The Southern Lights Holiday Festival has become a favorite holiday season activity for families and groups from around the area and the country.

Visitors have the chance to spend the night in the heart of Bluegrass horse country at the Kentucky Horse Park's Resort Campground.

The Kentucky Horse Park is also home to the National Horse Center, an ever-growing office complex of prestigious equine associations, commissions, organizations and services.

Every acre of the Kentucky Horse Park is dedicated to the horse and no matter the season, it is a fascinating place to visit. Truly an experience of a lifetime!

The History of the Park

The one thousand thirty-two-acre tract of land on which the Kentucky Horse Park now sits has been home to some of the finest Thoroughbred, Saddlebred and Standardbred horses bred in Kentucky. Horses have been on this ground for over 200 years with one Kentucky Derby winner, and numerous trotting horse champions being raised on these rolling Bluegrass hills. Those who have owned this land have played important roles in both the development of Kentucky and the Kentucky horse industry. It is for this reason and many others that the Commonwealth of Kentucky chose this land in 1972 to establish an educational theme park dedicated to the animal whose name has become synonymous with the Bluegrass State.

The story of the land begins in 1777 when then Governor of Virginia, Patrick Henry, granted 9,000 acres of land in the Kentucky Territory to his brother-in-law, Colonel William Christian, for his service in the French and Indian War. One three thousand-acre tract sat on the North Elkhorn Creek north of present-day Lexington. Colonel Christian also owned land on Beargrass Creek near present-day Louisville, where he moved his family in 1785. Unfortunately, he was killed the next year by marauding Indians at the age of forty-three. In his will he left 1,000 acres of the Elkhorn tract to his daughter Elizabeth and directed that the remainder be sold and used for the care and education of his younger children. Part of Elizabeth's original inheritance would become the Kentucky Horse Park but not before it was owned and lost by many prominent Kentuckians.

In 1805, Elizabeth and her husband Richard Dickinson, sold their 1,000 acres to her brother-in-law, Dr. Walter Warfield. Eventually Dr. Warfield would divide the property and sell 400 acres in 1816 to Matthew Flournoy, 400 acres in 1826 to Dr. William Richardson and 200 acres to Samuel Muir sometime in the 1820's.

Senorita Stud Farm c. 1905, picture includes the present-day Big Barn, Draft Horse Barn, Administrative Offices and Carriage Horse Barn.

Matthew Flournoy, a French Huguenot, came to Scott County from Virginia in 1790 and would purchase considerable land holdings in the Scott and Fayette county area. In his 1842 will he left his portion of the Christian tract to his son Victor. Matthew had named this section Walnut Hall after the family estate and chateau in France. After a fire destroyed the house his father built, Victor Flournoy constructed the present Walnut Hall residence in the late 1840s. After his death in 1866 and his wife's in 1879, Thoroughbred breeder, Major John Clark, purchased this section of land.

Major Clark was the first owner of Walnut Hall to extensively breed horses. However he did not continue his horse venture long, selling Walnut Hall in 1884 to Rudolph and Mary Weiser. They in turn would sell the farm to Lamon Vanderberg Harkness in 1891. Harkness would establish one of the most prominent Standardbred breeding farms in Kentucky and eventually reunite the original Christian tract under single ownership.

Dr. William H. Richardson purchased the remaining 400 acres of Warfield's land in 1826. Dr. Richardson had come to Kentucky with his parents in 1789. He received his medical training at the University of Pennsylvania and

would teach at the Medical School of Transylvania University in Lexington, the first college west of the Alleghenies. Dr. Richardson developed a beautiful country estate with a fourteen-room brick mansion, extensive gardens and a greenhouse, which he called Caneland. In 1839 he gave Caneland to his son Louis, who bred and raced Thoroughbreds. The Richardson family would be wiped out in Kentucky by the cholera epidemic that struck Lexington in the 1840s and by 1848 the land had been purchased by Eliphalet Muir, a grandson of Samuel Muir, who renamed the farm Caneland Stock Farm.

Muir and his wife Anne Boone, a grandniece of Daniel Boone, further developed the farm and specialized in raising Saddlebred horses. They were the first in the area to import European breeds to improve the breeding strain. With Muir's death the farm was sold to S. J. Salyers in order to divide the inheritance between Muir's many children.

Thoroughbred horses were again bred on the property, with one of Salyers' horses running in the first Kentucky Derby. Salyers also built the residence that is now used for offices by the Kentucky Horse Park. The house, which was completed in 1866, was built on the foundation of an older structure that had burned prior to the Civil War.

By 1890 the farm was again sold, this time to John D. Creighton. Creighton renamed the farm Ashland-Wilkes Farm and began raising and training trotting horses. He built the training track in 1897. He also built the oldest section of the Big Barn, the Draft Horse Barn and the Carriage Barn prior to the turn of the century. Yet again the land had to be sold in order to pay creditors.

For a short time, two Lexington bankers owned the farm. They leased the land to Colonel Milton Young, owner of McGrathiana Farm (now the University of Kentucky's Spindletop and Coldstream Farms). Young sent several of his Standardbred yearlings, raised on the property, to a New York auction, where an agent for Captain Sam S. Brown saw them. Captain Brown liked their looks so much that he purchased their home in 1902 in order to raise horses of a similar caliber.

A wealthy coal baron, Brown rebuilt the farm and named it Senorita Stud Farm, after one of his favorite mares. Brown stabled good stock at Senorita, with two Kentucky Derby winners, Buchanan (1884, part-owner) and Agile (1904). He built water towers (two still stand today) around the farm to pump fresh water to his horses from a spring that never ran dry. This was an innovation in a time when few people had running water. Brown would also be responsible for rebuilding the old Kentucky Association Racetrack in Lexington, which was eventually moved and became present day Keeneland Racecourse.

Brown was not in good health at the time he purchased the farm and in 1908 (following his death) the farm was again sold. The farm was offered at public auction and Lamon V. Harkness was the buyer. With this purchase Harkness reunited the original Christian tract.

Harkness developed Walnut Hall into one of the largest and best-known Standardbred farms in the country. It grew from 450 acres and 12 mares in 1894 to 2,000 acres and 100 mares in 1904. Harkness added the western portion of the Big Barn and built an indoor auction area, making it possible for Walnut Hall to be the first major

Salyers' House c. 1866

Kentucky Standardbred nursery to auction its yearlings on site.

After the death of Lamon V. Harkness in 1915, one daughter, Lela Harkness Edwards bought the interests of the other heirs. She and her husband, Dr. Ogden Edwards, Jr., would continue Walnut Hall Farm's success. After their deaths, the land was divided between their daughter, Kate Edwards Nichols, and their son's widow, Mary. In 1947, Mrs. Nichols continued to operate the farm as Walnut Hall Farm while Mary Edwards (then Mrs. Sherman Jenney) called her estate Walnut Hall Stud.

For decades, Central Kentucky's horse farms had provided an anchor for tourism in the Bluegrass. During the late 1960s, however, many horse farms had to close their doors to the public as a result of vandalism and increased labor costs. In response to this, Lexington horseman, John R. Gaines, suggested to members of the Kentucky Legislature that the Commonwealth of Kentucky should open a theme park dedicated to the horse, and the horse industry, as a way to gain back lost tourism revenue. His idea was to create a public attraction where visitors could experience a Kentucky horse farm and to maintain the identity of Lexington as the "Horse Capital of the World."

In 1970, the Kentucky Legislature approved a plan to purchase land and create just such a park in Fayette County. In April 1972, Mary Edwards Jenney sold her Walnut Hall Stud property to the Commonwealth of Kentucky for $2,700,000 to become the Kentucky Horse Park. In the summer of 1974, ground was officially broken by then Governor Wendell Ford. 1974 also marked the first horse-related special event to be held on the grounds, when the High Hope Steeplechase moved its annual one-day meet to the Park's newly constructed course.

Construction, renovation and planning progressed for the next four years. In 1975, the Park was chosen as the site of the 1978 World Three-Day Event Championship, the first equestrian world championship to ever take place in North America. On June 23, 1977, Man o' War and

African-American jockey Isaac Burns Murphy were reinterred at the Park and in April 1978, the campground became the first element of the new Park to open to the public.

The Kentucky Horse Park officially opened to the public on November 30, 1978. The final project cost $35,000,000. Fourteen original structures were renovated along with the construction of 23 new buildings, an interstate exit ramp, three bridges, a seven-acre lake, a resort campground, nine miles of paved roads, 27 miles of board fence, a one-mile steeplechase course, plus a cross-country course and dressage and stadium jumping areas.

In 1985, the Kentucky Horse Park Foundation was formed to expand and enhance the Kentucky Horse Park. Since its inception, funds provided by the Foundation have been instrumental in the improvement of the Park's equine competition facilities, making the Park one of the finest equine event facilities in North America. Through the Foundation, the Kentucky Horse Park hosts major fund-raisers such as the High Hope Steeplechase, held in May, and the Southern Lights Holiday Festival that draws thousands of visitors to the area and assists the Kentucky Horse Park in becoming a year-round attraction. In addition, the Foundation continues to fund various other projects which ensure the success of the Kentucky Horse Park for future generations.

Throughout the years the rolling hills and white plank fences of the Kentucky Horse Park have become the quintessential image of Kentucky and the horse industry. Today the Park welcomes nearly one million visitors annually and hosts a full schedule of world-class equestrian events as well as over 200 other special events. The Kentucky Horse Park has introduced thousands of people from around the world to the fascinating and exciting world of the horse and will continue to entertain and educate the public for years to come.

Walnut Hall Stud Farm's horse cemetery, located near the Big Barn.

Man o' War
and Isaac Burns Murphy

The heroic bronze statue of Man o' War stands on a pedestal just inside the entrance to the Kentucky Horse Park. It commands the attention of every visitor who enters the Park, just as the racehorse it memorializes commanded the eyes of all who witnessed his greatness on the track.

Man o' War was foaled on March 19, 1917 at August Belmont II's Nursery Stud, just outside Lexington. Samuel Riddle purchased Man o' War at the 1918 Saratoga yearling sales. He would totally dominate his peers during his two years on the track, winning 20 of his 21 starts. After his 3-year-old season, Man o' War was retired to stud at Riddle's Faraway Farm in Lexington. From 1921 until his death in 1947, he sired 379 foals; 291 of which went on to race, and 64 of these were stakes winners. War Admiral, his most famous son, won the 1937 Triple Crown and is buried near his sire at the memorial.

Sculpted by Herbert Haseltine, the statue was originally placed over Man o' War's grave at Faraway Farm. Prior to the Kentucky Horse Park's opening in 1978, the remains of Man o' War and statue were moved to their current location to symbolize the courage, strength and magnificence of all horses.

Isaac Burns Murphy, an outstanding African-American jockey of the 19th century, was born in Fayette County in 1861. During his career on the track he would win 628 races out of 1,412 starts, a winning percentage of 44%, a record which he still holds today. He died in 1896 after winning three Kentucky Derbies. In 1977, Murphy's body was reinterred near the Man o' War memorial after his grave was located in an abandoned cemetery in Lexington.

Visitor Information Center

Nearly one million tourists, horse enthusiasts and school children visit the Kentucky Horse Park each year. All are welcomed to the Park in the Visitor Information Center. Here the introductory film, "Thou Shalt Fly Without Wings," is shown throughout the day. This award-winning film serves as an introduction to the fascinating world of the horse to which the Kentucky Horse Park is dedicated. Visitor will also find exhibits on the United States Pony Club and the Bureau of Land Management's Adopt-A-Horse or Burro Program, as well as the Park's Gift Shop.

Promise and Frisky Filly by Gwen Reardon welcome visitors to the Park.

The Park Gift Shop offers a wide variety of unique equine gifts, original art and souvenirs.

The International Museum of the Horse is the world's largest and most comprehensive equestrian museum.

Museums

Throughout five thousand years of domestication, no animal has had a more significant impact on human history than the horse. From the tiny first horse, Eohippus, to the profusion of breeds and equine activities that exists today, the International Museum of the Horse traces the history of man's most steadfast partner with its extensive collection of artifacts and information. Within the Museum you will find the 560 piece Calumet Farm trophy collection, a collection of thirty 19th century horse-drawn carriages and racing vehicles along with exhibits about the draft horse in America, horseracing in Japan and the horse breeds of the world. The 58,000 square foot museum supports a comprehensive education program which annually host over 32,000 school children; a 3,000 volume research library and a 10,000 square foot special exhibitions area which hosts internationally significant exhibits on the horse and features artwork by some of the world's finest equestrian artists.

The American Saddlebred Museum and Gift Shop, located adjacent to the visitor's parking area, offers visitors an opportunity to experience one of the world's most exciting breeds of show horse. A native Kentucky breed and one of the oldest registered breeds in the United States, the Saddlebred is featured in an array of unique exhibits including Don Stafford's famous one-of-a-kind brass-fixtured show tack room and the award-winning multi-image theater show, Saddlebred for America. The Museum also houses the world's largest collection of George Ford Morris paintings, the breed's most comprehensive library and the largest collection of Saddlebred gifts, clothing and merchandise.

*Bask++ by Edwin Bogucki

Calumet Farm Trophy Collection

Supreme Sultan, by artist, Patricia Crane, welcomes visitors to the American Saddlebred Museum.

Working Horse Farm

The Kentucky Horse Park introduces thousands of visitors to the horse and the daily tasks of running a successful horse farm. As many as 100 horses representing 40 different breeds reside at the Park during the year, all needing daily care and attention. The Park staff is knowledgeable in all aspects of horse care and is available to answer any question. Visitors can discover the ancient craft of horse shoeing and watch as the horses are groomed and saddled in preparation for the show ring or harnessed for a trolley tour. Here the world of the horse can be experienced first hand.

The residents of the Hall of Champions are presented to the public three times daily (Mid-March-October).

Hall of Champions

Some of the world's greatest equine competitors reside at the Hall of Champions. Originally the stallion barn for Walnut Hall Stud Farm, it is now home to Thoroughbred racing greats John Henry, Bold Forbes and the legendary Cigar, who collectively have career earnings of over $17 million. Quarter Horse racing champion Sgt. Pepper Feature, World Grand

Champion Five-Gaited American Saddlebred CH Sky Watch, two-time Standardbred Horse of the Year Cam Fella, and one of the fastest pacers of all time Staying Together have also retired in style here. The Hall of Champions Cemetery serves as the final resting-place for former resident champions Rambling Willie, CH Imperator and Forego.

24

CH Sky Watch, in 1988, became the oldest horse ever to win the Five-Gaited World's Grand Championship, his fourth such win.

Retired to the Park in 1999, Cigar finished his racing career with a record of 19 wins in 33 starts and earnings of $9,999,815.

Bold Forbes won the Kentucky Derby in 1976 and is the oldest living Derby winner.

Cam Fella, "The Pacing Machine," won 28 consecutive races and in 1983 retired as the richest horse in harness racing history.

One of the best American Quarter Horse racers is Sgt. Pepper Feature. In 1982 he claimed the title of World Champion Quarter Running Horse.

John Henry, owned by Samuel Rubin, won seven Eclipse Awards and was the All-Time Leading Money Winner at the time of his retirement in July 1985. John Henry is the oldest resident at the Hall of Champions.

On June 19, 1993, Staying Together, posted the fastest race mile, to date, in harness history at 1:48.2 in the Driscoll Series at the Meadowlands.

The colorful and exciting Parade of Breeds is presented twice daily (Mid-March-October) in the Breeds Barn show ring.

Parade of Breeds

English Shire

Visitors have the opportunity to see over 40 different breeds of horse from around the world at the Kentucky Horse Park. English Shires, Connemara Ponies, American Miniatures, Tennessee Walking Horses, Arabians, Norwegian Fjord Horses, and of course, Thoroughbreds can be seen at work and at play throughout the Park. The Parade of Breeds offers an opportunity to see and learn about some of these horse breeds. Handlers and riders, in native costume or proper show attire, demonstrate the special characteristics of the horses as an announcer tells of the history and uses of the breed. Following the Parade, visitors are invited to go ringside to get close to the horses and talk with the riders. The Parade is proudly sponsored by *Equus Magazine*, the official publication of the Kentucky Horse Park.

Icelandic Pony

American Miniature

Connemara Pony

Arabian

American Quarter Horse

Trakehner

Morgan

Norwegian Fjord Horses

Thoroughbred

Lipizzan

Friesian

Draft Horses, Carriage Horses, and Horseback Rides

Nothing evokes the grandeur of the golden age of horsemanship more than the image of a matched pair of horses pulling a fine carriage through the countryside. The Draft Horse and Carriage Horse Barns transport the visitor back to that era. Here the visitor can discover the finer points of harnessing and driving heavy and light horse. The Draft Horse Barn is one of the few places in the world where you can see all of the major draft breeds, Shires, Percherons, Belgians, Clydesdales, Suffolk Punch, Haflingers and Mammoth Mules, under one roof. The Carriage Horse Barn is home to fine teams of Gelderlanders, Arabians, Morgans and Norwegian Fjord Horses.

The draft horses can be seen throughout the Park pulling the daily Horse Drawn Tour while the carriage horses take visitors on a more intimate ride in a turn of the century surrey. In the winter, they may even be seen pulling a sleigh through the newly fallen snow. Adults and children alike can also get close to the horses by taking a scenic horseback ride around the grounds or on their first pony ride.

Events & Shows

The Kentucky Horse Park is the premier equine event facility in the United States. Throughout the year over 70 horse shows, three-day events, rodeos, polo matches and steeplechase competitions are held on the grounds along with over 200 other special events. Annually the Park hosts events like the Rolex Kentucky Three-Day Event (the only four-star three-day competition in North America), the High Hope Steeplechase, the Egyptian Event, the Kentucky Fall Classic Saddlebred Show and Breyerfest. However, horse shows are not the only thing one can experience at the Park. Dog shows, cross-country track meets, concerts, and soccer tournaments fill the Park's calendar.

The Rolex Kentucky Three-Day Event is always scheduled to include the last weekend of April.

Dressage

Cross-country

Stadium jumping

High Hope Steeplechase

Polo

U.S. Pony Club Events

Southern Lights

The holiday season comes alive at the Kentucky Horse Park with the "Southern Lights: Spectacular Sights on Holiday Nights" Christmas light display. Named one of the top twenty holiday attractions in the South, the Southern Lights Holiday Festival has become a holiday tradition for families throughout the area. The spectacle of Southern Lights follows a four-mile route with thousands of twinkling lights showing the joy of the Christmas season along with equestrian scenes and, of course, Santa's sleigh and reindeer. Inside special holiday entertainment is provided along with arts and crafts for those special Christmas gifts. And no visit would be complete without taking time to have a picture made with Santa.

National headquarters for the American Horse Shows Association, the governing body for equestrian sport in the United States.

National Horse Center

In the early 1980s, the Kentucky Horse Park began to approach horse organizations and breed associations in order to establish a complex of national equine-related organizations. The American Saddlebred Horse Association was the first such group to move its new national headquarters on the grounds in 1985 and was soon followed by the opening of the American Saddlebred Museum. Since then the National Horse Center has become the home to many of the most influential equine associations, commissions, organizations and services within the horse industry. This new and growing office complex is home for the American Horse Shows Association, the American Association of Equine Practitioners, the American Farrier's Association, the American Hackney Horse Association, the American Hanoverian Association, the American Saddlebred Horse Association, the American Saddlebred Museum, the American Youth Horse Council, Central Kentucky Riding for the Handicapped, Equestrian Events, Inc., the Kentucky Thoroughbred Association, the Kentucky Thoroughbred Owners & Breeders, the Kentucky Racing Commission, The Pyramid Society, the United Professional Horseman's Association, the United States Polo Association and the United States Pony Club.

The Campground was the first attraction at the Park to open to the public in April 1978.

Campground

The Kentucky Horse Park Campground is one of the finest in the South offering campers the best in Southern hospitality. The Campground is open year-round offering 260 campsites complete with electrical and water hookups, paved pads, fire rings and picnic tables as well as primitive camping areas. The resort campground is a full service facility offering many extras including a grocery and souvenir shop, two bathhouses, laundromats and two dump stations. Recreational activities include lighted courts for tennis and basketball, a junior Olympic-size swimming pool, horseshoes and playgrounds for the children.

肯德基州馬公園
肯州牧馬場生活的寫實經驗

肯德基州牧馬公園具草原特色的對外開放二十日公園開園自以來，始終秉持的活動自一月一日設一月一日兼施無三貫，園內多元化和知識性，教藉著景，此外原野牧場背此外原野牧場有所。此外原野牧場有邊闊原野牧場的烘托下，游客可有機會觀察不同品種馬的生活動態。本地的二十宗旨本地公園為肯州州民提供了一個融和精神與舊，新代化與現代化世界上持八年十一月的活動自世界各地的知識性，教藉著肯德基州特有的烘托下，游客可有機會觀察不同品種馬的生活動態。

肯德基馬公園佔地超過一千英畝，可盡情奔馳，並讓游客所扮演的重要角色。對馬有興趣的人，只要來到本公園參觀一天，便可留下終身難忘的回憶。讓馬兒在此類人類歷史上對馬有興趣的人，只要來到本公園參觀一天，便可留下終身難忘的回憶。

本公園的進口處有一座銅馬雕像，底下埋葬了著名賽馬"勇士"的英魂，游客通常在此停駐瞻仰。在游客服務中心內，每天都有播放"天馬行空"的園區介紹影片，游客可透過這部精彩生動的影片一窺駿馬世界的奧妙。

公園內有兩座世界水準級的博物館，一座是"國際馬博物館"，另一座是"美國騎術博物館"。"國際馬博物館"是世界上最具宏規，並且一流之先進的馬術博物館。透過館內的人馬具不同的資料與博物館裏育種的馬種，參觀者可聽到各種具有不同的資料與收藏品。"美國騎術博物館"則專門介紹肯州育種的馬種馬，隨著此領進在美國歷史上所造成的影響力。現代間的有趣故事為大眾展現出在美國歷史上所造成的影響。步種馬被引進入精彩的賽馬場歷史上。另外，此館還為大眾展現出肯州育種的馬種被引進後在美國的蹄步，參觀者將世界面馬引睹。

步出博物館，游客們可在戶外目睹肯德基牧馬場的每日生活寫實面。園區

裏的工作人員會向大家示範每天給上百四馬所做的例行工作，其中有包括飼養，梳洗，和運動等項目。游客們同時可在鐵匠示範店裏看到園區獸醫為馬兒做鐵蹄的古老技藝。

本公園亦提供游客騎馬走小徑或是乘馬車游園的機會，另外，游客們也可參加各種不同的教育活動。每年的四月到十月之間，園區內到處充滿了熱鬧的聲音與色彩，在種馬廄裏將有一天兩場的品種馬展，向游客們介紹四十多種本公園育養的品種馬。"冠軍名馬廳"則是各種優良馬的大本營，在此廳內游客可有一天三次的機會觀賞歷年來比賽得獎的純種馬，標準馬和賽馬等等名星馬隊游行活動。

除了每天的固定活動之外，本公園亦主辦世界級的騎馬術比賽，例如一年一度的勞力世肯德基三日活動，越野障礙賽馬，和埃及活動。此外，本公園還主辦足球公開賽，優良犬種展，音樂會和"老肯德基之夜"等不同貫穿全年的活動。

聖誕節期間，本園裝飾有五彩壯觀的主會地燈飾，展現以聖誕節和馬術有關的嘉年華題。這個標名為"南方燈飾"的應節燈展，在冬季裏吸引了各地的居民來欣賞。

本公園亦有營區提供游客露營過夜。

肯德基馬公園是"國家馬中心"的故鄉，專為不同享富名聲的馬術協會和組職提供服務。

肯德基馬公園每一寸土地都是奉獻給與馬有關的活動。這是一個不分季節的游覽聖地，來此的游客都能嘗試到一生難忘的經驗。

ケンタッキー・ホースパーク

ケンタッキーの牧場を生で体験

ケンタッキー・ホースパークは、古いものと新しいものとが融合する所です。馬の産地「ブルーグラス」（ケンタッキー州の愛称）の輝かしい伝統を残しながら、現代的な「革新」をも大切にしているのです。このホースパークは、1978年11月30日に開園して以来こんにちまで、確固たる目標を守り通してきました。

　「馬のテーマ・パークとして、ケンタッキーから、そして世界中から、ここを訪れる人々に、質の高い情報とリクリエーション、そして学ぶ場を提供します。馬だけに話題を絞った、世界で唯一のテーマ・パークとして、訪れる人々に、さまざまな種類の馬の、ありのままの日常を見ていただきます」

一千エーカー（およそ４千平方キロ）以上に及ぶ広大な土地が、もっぱら馬と、そして人類史における馬の役割を示すために使われているのです。馬に関心のある方ならば、どなたにとっても、このパークでの一日の経験が生涯の思い出になることでしょう。

ここを訪れる人はまず、大きなブロンズの像に出迎えられます。これは伝説的な「マン・ノ・ウォー」の墓碑なのです。インフォメーション・センターにおいて毎日上映されているフィルム、『羽なくて飛べ』は、訪れる人々を素晴らしい馬の世界に誘います。

世界的なレベルの二つの博物館が、パークの敷地内にあります。「インターナショナル・ミュージアム・オブ・ホース」そして「アメリカン・サドルホース・ミュージアム」です。「インターナショナル・ミュージアム・オブ・ホース」は、世界で最も大きく、最も内容の濃い、馬の博物館です。ここでは、馬にまつわる興味深い話や、人との関りが紹介されています。傑出した情報と工芸品のコレクションに加えて、最新のテクノロジーが、まさにユニークで楽しい博物館の体験を演出しています。「アメリカン・サドルホース・ミュージアム」は、「アメリカン・サドルブレッド」と呼ばれる、唯一ケンタッキー産の品種に特化した博物館です。ここでは、この歴史的価値のある馬の、エキサイティングなショーをお楽しみ下さい。

博物館の外側では、ケンタッキーの牧場での日々の営みを見ることができます。百頭以上もの馬の餌付けや世話や訓練を

しているのはホースパークのスタッフです。蹄鉄師の作業場の、光景や響きをお楽しみ下さい。金鎚の技術や、古くから伝わる装蹄の技をご覧になることができます。

ホースパークは、誰でもが参加できる体験も用意しております。乗馬、そして馬引きのトロリーや、馬車によるパーク内ツアー、数々の学習用プログラムなどです。４月から１０月までのホースパークでは、「ブリーズ・バーン」のグループが日に二回、様々な色合いと音楽の楽しいショーをお目にかけます。これは、このパーク内にいる、個性ある歴史と特色を持った、約４０の異なった種類の中から選び抜かれた馬たちによるパレードです。「ホール・オブ・チャンピオンズ」はサラブレッド、スタンダードブレッド、クウォーターホースといった馬のレースや、過去のショーにおけるスターたちを紹介する、いわばエリートたちのホームグラウンドです。毎日三回、ショーが行われます。

これらに加えて、ホースパークでは、世界的なレベルの馬の競技会が行なわれています。ロレックス・ケンタッキー・スリーデイや、ハイホープ障害、エジプシャン・イベントといった、年一回の恒例行事などです。またホースパークでは、サッカー・トーナメントやドッグ・ショー、演奏会や「オールド・ケンタッキー・ナイト」などの催しが、年間を通して開催されています。クリスマスの季節には、クリスマス飾りと馬のディスプレイを彩る、目を見張るような光のショーが行われます。「サザンライツ・ホリデー・フェスティバル」は、この地域や合衆国中の、ご家族やグループの方々に人気の催し物になっています。

「ケンタッキー・ホースパーク・キャンプ場」では、馬の里「ブルーグラス」のまっただ中で一夜を過ごすという体験をすることもできます。

ケンタッキー・ホースパークは、「ナショナル・ホースセンター」の根拠地でもあります。ここには、馬に関する数々の協会や委員会、組織や団体が置かれています。

「ケンタッキー・ホースパーク」のどの場所も、馬のために捧げられています。そこは、季節を問わず訪れることができる、魅惑の世界です。一生の思い出となることに、間違いありません！

Le Kentucky Horse Park
Une véritable expérience au sein de la Ferme Equestre du Kentucky

Le Kentucky Horse Park est un mélange d'ancien et de neuf , respectant à la fois, les traditions honorées du Bluegrass horse country (Etat de l'Herbe Bleue) et les innovations modernes. Officiellement ouvert au public le 30 novembre 1978, le Parc est resté fidèle à ses objectifs d'origine.

...le but du Parc est d'offrir aux habitants du Kentucky et aux visiteurs du monde entier, une expérience à la fois éducative et récréative de qualité, ayant pour thème le cheval. En tant qu'unique parc au monde dédié au cheval, celui-ci offre aux visiteurs la chance d'admirer une grande variété de races de chevaux, dans leurs exercices quotidiens, sur fonds du Kentucky horse farm, une ferme magnifiquement préservée.

Le Kentucky Horse Park est un endroit fascinant où plus de 3,5 hectares de terre sont consacrées aux chevaux et au rôle important qu'ils ont joué dans l'histoire de l'Humanité. Pour les admirateurs de chevaux, une journée au parc est une expérience inoubliable.

Les visiteurs sont accueillis dans le Parc par une immense statue représentant la tombe du légendaire Man o' War. Le monde fascinant du cheval débute avec un film passionant intitulé, «Thou Shalt Fly Without Wings », présenté quotidiennement au Centre d'Informations des Visiteurs.

Deux musées de classe mondiale se trouvent sur les terres du Parc : The International Museum of the Horse et The American Saddle Horse Museum. The International Museum of the Horse est le plus grand et le plus complet des musées équestres au monde dédié à l'Histoire du Cheval et à sa relation avec l'homme. Le visiteur profite d'une expérience unique et agréable grâce à une technologie de pointe qui vient compléter une collection étourdissante d'informations et d'objets. The American Saddle Horse Museum, principalement consacré à la race native du Kentucky, the American Saddlebred, emportera le visiteur dans le monde excitant de l'arène du spectacle avec cette espèce qui a joué un rôle important dans l'histoire.

Au-delà des murs du musée, chacun pourra assister aux tâches quotidiennes de la ferme équestre du Kentucky. Observez le personnel du Parc accomplir leurs travaux de routine pour nourrir, panser et excercer plus d'une centaines de chevaux.

Arrêtez-vous devant la boutique du maréchal-ferrant et appréciez une démonstration de son art : martèlement du fer et pratique ancienne du ferrage.

Le visiteur aura l'opportunité de faire un tour en charette, en trolley tiré par des chevaux, en équipage sur les terres du Parc ou encore de participer à un des nombreurx programmes éducatifs. Du mois d'avril et jusqu'en octobre, le Parc se remplit de joie de vivre et de fébrilité avec l'arène du spectacle. Le Breeds Barn accueille deux fois par jour en son sein, la Parade of Breeds (Parade des Races) : une présentation d'une sélection de chevaux qui apporte un éclairage sur l'histoire unique et le caractéristique de plus de 40 espèces différentes de chevaux résidant au Parc. Le Hall of Champions est, trois fois par jour, le foyer d'exposition de chevaux d'élite représentant des Thorouhgbred (Pur-Sang anglais), Standardbred (Trotteur américain) et Quarter Horse (coureur du quarter de mile) encore en course ou des anciennes étoiles.

En plus de ces activités quotidiennes, le Parc est l'hôte, tout au long de l'année, de compétitions équestres mondiales , d'évènements annuels comme le Rolex Kentucky Three-Day Event, le High Hope Steeplechase et l'Egyptian Event. Le parc accueille également des tournois de football, des expositions canines, des programmes de concerts et le Old Kentucky Night. La saison de Noel débute avec des illuminations spectaculaires mettant à la fois en vedette Noel et des exhibitions équestres. Le Southern Lights Holiday Festival est devenu l'une des activités favorites des vacances de noel pour les familles et les groupes des environs et du pays entier.

Les visiteurs auront aussi la chance de passer la nuit au coeur du Bluegrass horse country sur le terrain de camping du Parc.

Le Kentucky Horse Park est également le foyer du National Horse Center, un complexe de bureaux toujours grandissant réunissant des associations équines, des commissions, organisations et services.

Chaque hectare du Kentucky Horse Park est dédié au cheval et quelque soit la saison, c'est un endroit fascinant à visiter. C'est véritablement une expérience inoubliable !

Der Kentucky Horse Park
Eine Echte Kentucky Pferdezüchteri Erfahrung

Der Kentucky Horse Park ist eine Mischung aus dem Alten und Neuen mit Rücksicht auf die geehrten Traditionen des Bluegrass Pferdelandes und die modernen Innovationen. Seit der offiziellen Eröffnung am 30. November 1978 realisiert der Park seinem erklärten Ziel

> eine Erfahrung voller Qualität, Information, Spaß und Bildung, mit dem Pferd als Thema, für alle Kentuckianer(innen) und Besuchern aus der ganzen Welt. Als einzigen zum-Pferde-gewidmeten Park der Welt bietet er seinen Besuchern die Chance eine Züchtungsvielfalt in ihrem Alltagsleben wegen einem Hintergrund von himmlisch gepflegtem Kentucky Pferdezüchterei zu sehen an.

Der Kentucky Horse Park ist eine faszinierende Ort mit mehr als ein Tausend Aker Grundflächenmaß, gewidmet zum Pferde und seiner wichtigen Rolle in der Geschichte des Mannes. Ein Tag im Park heisst für jeden Mensch, der das Pferd verehrt, eine grosse Erfahrung im Leben.

Begrüsst sind Parkbesuchern von einer riesen Bronzestatue, die das Grab dem legendären Man-o-War designiert. Die faszinierende Welt des Pferdes wird täglich durch den erregenden Einführungsfilm „Du Sollst Ohne Flügeln Fliegen" im Besuchersinformationzentrum lebendig gemacht.

Zwei weltklassige Museums sind im Park zu finden, das „International Museum of the Horse" und das „American Saddle Horse Museum". Das International Museum of the Horse ist das grösste und beinhaltendister Pferdemuseum der Welt, gewidmet von der Erzählung der intrigierenden Geschichte vom Pferde und seiner Verbindung zum Mann. Die neueste Technologie ergänzt eine ausgezeichnete Sammlung von Information und gesammelten Werken und Gegenständer aus vergangener Zeit, welche ein einmaliges und angenehmes Museumerlebnis erschaffen. Das American Saddle Horse Museum konzentriert sich auf das einzigste eingeborenen Rasse Kentuckys der Amerikanischen Sattelzucht, und nimmt zeigt Besuchern der begeisternden Welt dem Ausstellungsring mit dieser historisch beeindruckzuckender Zucht.

Jenseits der Museummauer kann man die alltäglichen Arbeiten einer Pferdezüchterei besichtigen. Man kann zuschauen wie die Parkmitarbeiter(innen) die täglichen Aufgaben wie füttern, striegeln und trainieren von den mehr als ein hundert Pferde des Parkes. Sehen und hören Sie die Klänge einem

Schmiede wo der Hufschmied des Parkes seine Schmiedekunst vorstellt und die uralte Art von Hufe beschlagen praktiziert.

Der Park bietet jedem die Gelegenheit an beim Pfadreiten, beim pferdgezogener Wagenfahrt, bei Kutschenfahrt durch den Parkgrund oder beim Teilnehmen an einem der vielen Ausbildungsprogramme echten Kontakt mit den Pferde zu bekommen. Von April bis October werden die Farben, Klänge und Aufregung dem Ausstellungsring zweimal täglich durch die Präsentation der „Parade of Breeds" (Rassenparade), eine Ausstellung von ausgewählten Pferde, die die einzigartige Geschichte und den Charakter der 40 verschiedenen Rassen, die im Park leben, hervorheben. Die Halle der Meister ist für eine Elitegruppe ehemaliger Rennpferde das Zuhause. Diese Gruppe beinhaltet drei Rassen: Vollblut, Standardrasse und Rasse Quarter Horse, die dreimal täglich im Ausstellungsring vorgestellt werden.

Außer den täglichen Aktivitäten präsentiert der Park einen kompletten Zeitplan weltklassiger Pferdewettkämpfe wie den jährlichen „Rolex Kentucky Three-Day Event," das „High Hope Steeplechase" (ein Hindernisrennen) und den „Egyptian Event." Im Park finden auch Fußballturniere, Hundeausstellungen, Konzerte und „Old Kentucky Night" Programme durch das ganze Jahr statt. In der Weihnactssaison wird mit einer aufsehend erregenden Lichtenanlage die Weihnachts- und Pferdewelt lebendig gemacht. Das „Southern Lights Holiday Festival" ist eine beliebte Weihnachtsaktivität für Familien und Gruppen aus der Gegend und aus dem Land geworden.

Besucher haben auch die Chance eine Nacht im Herzen des Bluegrasspferdelandes aud dem Kentucky Horse Park Campingplatz zu verbringen.

Der Kentucky Horse Park ist auch für das National Horse Center, einen immer wachsenden Komplex aus Buros prestigevollen Organizationen und Dienste.

Jeder Meter von dem Kentucky Horse Park ist dem Pferde gewidmet und egal um welche Jahreszeit dieser Ort besucht wird, es ist ein faszinierendes Erlebnis. Eine echte Lebenserfahrung!

El Parque y La Finca de Caballos de Kentucky
es Una Verdadera Experiencia

El Parque de Caballos de Kentucky es una mezcla de lo viejo y lo nuevo, respetando ambas, dando honor a la tradición de la grama azul del país de los caballos y la innovación moderna. Oficialmente fue abierto al publico el 30 de noviembre de 1978, el Parque hoy en día continua sirviendo el mismo proposito"... el de proveer una experiencia informativa, recreativa y educativa, teniendo los caballos como tema, para la gente de Kentucky y visitantes de todo el mundo. Siendo el único parque en el mundo dedicado a los caballos, ofrece a los visitantes la oportunidad de mirar una gran variedad de diferentes razas de caballos en su rutina diaria, teniendo como panorama una granja de caballos mantenida impecablemente."

El Parque de Caballos de Kentucky es un lugar fascinante, donde más de mil acres de tierra están dedicados a los caballos y al importante rol que estos han jugado en la historia de la humanidad, un día en al Parque puede ser una experiencia única en la vida.

Los visitantes son recibidos en el parque por una gran estatua de bronce que marca la tumba del legendario caballo "Man o' War. (Caballo Luchador) El mundo fascinante de los caballos toma vida a través de una película introductora "Volarán Sin Alas," presentada diariamente a los visitantes en el Centro de Información.

Los dos museos de primera clase se pueden encontrar en el Parque, El Museo Internacional de Caballos y el Museo de Montura Americana. En el Museo Internacional de los Caballos los visitantes tienen la oportunidad de explorar los 58 millones de años de la historia ecuestre. Es el museo más grande y completo del mundo; dedicado a contar la intrigante historia de los caballos y su relación con la humanidad. La más avanzada tecnología ayuda a complementar una extraordinaria colección de artefactos informativos, produciendo un verdadero gozo de una experiencia única en el museo.

El Museo de Montura Americana se concentra en las razas nativas de Kentucky, llevando a los visitantes al excitante mundo de las competencias y la influencia histórica de esta raza.

Más allá de las paredes del Museo, se puede ser testigo del trabajo que se realiza todos los días en la granja de caballos de Kentucky. Ver como el personal realiza su trabajo diario de alimentar, cepillar y ejercitar a más de cien caballos. Experimente, vea y oiga los sonidos de la herrería mientras el artesano del Parque muestra su arte trabajando el hierro y produciendo herraduras como se hacia en tiempos pasados y actuales.

De abril a octubre el Parque se reaviva con el color, sonidos y el entusiasmo del circulo de exhibiciones, y en las Barracas se presentan dos veces al día, un desfile de Caballos de Raza, una presentación de caballos escogidos enfatizando el carácter e historia de cada una de las cuarenta razas diferentes que residen en el Parque. La Sala de Campeones es donde residen un grupo elite de caballos que representan las diferentes clases de competencias, tales como: Thoroughbred, Standardbred y Quarter, y también en el círculo de exhibiciones se muestran las estrellas competidoras del pasado tres veces al día. Además de las actividades diarias, el Parque presenta un horario completo de competencias ecuestres de primera clase y una variedad de eventos especiales durante todo el año.

El Parque ofrece a todos la oportunidad de una experiencia real con los caballos por un sendero o un paseo en una carreta halada por caballos o un paseo en carruaje por el Parque o participación en uno de los muchos programas educacionales. Los visitantes también tienen la oportunidad de pasar la noche en el corazón del estado conocido como el país de los caballos y la Grama Azul.

La temporada Navideña revive con un gran espectáculo de luces mostrando temas navideños y ecuestres. El Festival Sureño de Luces se ha convertido en una de las actividades más populares para familias y grupos de el área cercana y del país.

El Parque de Caballos de Kentucky es también el hogar del Centro Nacional de Caballos, un complejo de muy prestigiadas asociaciones ecuestres, comisiones, organizaciones y servicios, el cual crece y crece cada día más.

Cada acre del Parque de Caballos de Kentucky está dedicado a los caballos y sin importar la estación, es siempre un sitio fascinante para visitar y verdaderamente una experiencia única en la vida.